T0164605

BEAUTIFUL TROUBLE

CRAB ORCHARD SERIES IN POETRY

First Book Award

BEAUTIFUL TROUBLE Amy Fleury

Crab Orchard Review

&

Southern Illinois University Press

CARBONDALE

Printed in the United States of America

07   4 3   ˙

The Crab Orchard Series in Poetry is a joint publishing venture of
Southern Illinois University Press and *Crab Orchard Review*. This series
has been made possible by the generous support of the Office of the President of
Southern Illinois University and the Office of the Vice Chancellor for Academic
Affairs and Provost at Southern Illinois University Carbondale.

Crab Orchard Series in Poetry Editor: Jon Tribble
First Book Award Judge for 2003: Judy Jordan

Library of Congress Cataloging-in-Publication Data

Fleury, Amy, 1970–
 Beautiful trouble / Amy Fleury.
  p. cm. — (Crab Orchard series in poetry)
 I. Title. II. Series: Crab Orchard series in poetry.
 PS3606. L489B43 2004
 811'.6—dc22
 ISBN 0-8093-2598-5 (pbk. : alk. paper)   2004003980

Printed on recycled paper. ♻

The paper used in this publication meets the minimum requirements of
American National Standard for Information Sciences—Permanence of Paper
for Printed Library Materials, ANSI Z39.48-1992. ∞

for my folks

Contents

Acknowledgments

Grateful acknowledgment is made to the editors of the following publications, where some of these poems originally appeared:

Briar Cliff Review—"Mercy at Home"

Flint Hills Review—"Burning Back," "Remedy"

Kansas English—"About Rose Ida," "To Spit and Hone," "Penance: Reading to a Shut-In"

The Laurel Review—"Aurelia Waiting," "Always Girl"

Mid-American Poetry Review—"Wherever the Dancing Is Done," "Rhythm"

Midwest Quarterly—"Commotions of the Flesh," "The Fugitive Eve"

North American Review—"Fifth Grade"

Plains Song Review—"Nemaha County Nocturne"

Platte Valley Review—"Things Familiar"

Prairie Schooner—"Backroad," "Threshing," "A Prayer for Intercession"

Red Rock Review—"Consider the Thunder," "Sonnet for Dissonance," "Homestead," "The Thirsting Hours"

The Review—"Almanac"

South Dakota Review—"Covenant"

Southeast Review—"Pink," "Papier-Mâché Jupiter"

Southern Poetry Review—"At Twenty-Eight"

Talking River Review—"The Wound You Need"

Willow Review—"Epithalamion for a Maiden Aunt"

"Jazz Rhapsody" appeared in the liner notes of Michael Jefry Stevens's CD *Portraits in Red* (Cactus Records, 2001).

"Supplications to the Blessed Mother" appeared in *Place of Passage: Contemporary Catholic Poetry* (Story Line Press, 2000).

Special thanks go to Allen Braden, Tom Averill, Neil Connelly, Dan Daly, Robert Stein, Dan Glynn, Steve and Harriet Lerner, Martin and Barbara Taylor, Elizabeth Dodd, Jonathan Holden, Mark Fleury, Jon Tribble, Judy Jordan, and Karl Kageff. I am most deeply grateful to John Wood, friend and mentor.

I also wish to express my gratitude to the MacDowell Colony for a residency, as well as to the family of Nadya Aisenberg for the support of the colony fellowship.

O N E

Always Girl

That girl,
always a string bean child
fretting at her mama's skirts.
Her time will come, sorry to say.

She trips across pasture tugging
that grubby-toed baby doll,
always blond, always girl.
She hides in the corncrib
that cradles puckered ears,
afraid of those kernels that hang
like brown teeth on wicked gums.
She spins, she spins, dizzy and silly.
That girl, she stands by the creek,
shivering ribs and bruised and bony knees,
sipping thimbles of sunshine, she does.

Soon she will wake from her moon-blessed sleep,
ripe with morning. That girl will find
stained panties and her own worried hems.
And on some porch, she will sit and sweat and squint
and shuck her corn with blistered thumbs.
She'll conjure thunder and shuck that corn.

Consolation

Once there was a walnut tree that shook its sorrows onto our house.
At night we could hear them clatter to the roof,
tumbling over shingles, wobbling down the pitch.
In the bellowing wind, the tree bent beneath the eaves.
Its branches tapped and scraped at our window
until my brother too unfurled from the tight husk of sleep.
What were we to do? A boy, a girl, adrift in our beds,
washed in the shadows of a tree bereft.

On autumn days its roots followed me all over the yard.
Hulls lay about. Squirrels pillaged the hollow snouts.
We raked the torn leaves into piles,
and in the chilled evenings they burned.
The smoke lifted from loam to limbs;
ash settled on our shadows, our coats.
What would we make of a life both blighted and blessed?
There was trouble all around and everywhere little mercies.

Penance: Reading to a Shut-In

For a while I was enamored of such a life,
of sealed doors and the shades drawn.
I arrived in the afternoons, mittened and scarved,
bringing in winter and a book.
She'd sat there for years in her shawl
on account of frailty and a bruised womb.
She was delicate, a chipped dish shelved,
waiting and waiting to be used.
Her thin-paged Bible balanced
like a platter in my lap
as I traced each chapter,
each martyr with an inky thumb.
And in this way we passed the drowsy, gray hours.

But I wanted to comb her white web of hair
and tell her the stories I had learned
of spies and witches and children lost in woods.
When camphor and furnace soured, I left her house
with my pockets full of fists.
I crossed the school yard, hunched in my coat,
scraping worn hopscotch chalk with my boots.
That street was littered with sticks and leaves,
and the wind numbed my legs, chafed my face.
Those days I was a child shriven,
a loosed girl, running home.

Papier-Mâché Jupiter

Torn strips of the Kansas City Star, gray news
   from 1979, farm crisis headlines dredged in glue,
      Jimmy Carter's crumpled face pasted

on a yellow balloon. Layer on layer, she
   bandaged it with the worry of a maker.
      In the opened book was all she knew

of Jupiter—a gaseous ball, distorted and large,
   home to a scarlet, ongoing storm. From across
      the night, songs came over the radio

into her family's patient house, songs to dance to,
   if you cared to, but she hummed instead.
      Her face, a curious moon, concentrated

above striations of drying tempera paint, glossy
   bronzes and pearled blues. This is how a world
      gets born in a kitchen's beneficent light,

a churning wonder come from an accident of dust,
   some child's science project, a flimsy planet
      unsuitable for orbit, puckered navel poking out.

Through the window she could see the wide plain,
   like an earnest and well-made table holding up
      the heavens while she held this new Jupiter.

To lift up a celestial thing, such a satisfying shape,
   and to turn it in the blunt span of her hands
      was proof enough of her own modest divinity.

Fifth Grade

She rode a short bus, little loaf of bread on wheels,
which let her out at the front steps of her red brick school.
The classroom smelled like pencil lead and minty paste,
and lacy, paper snowflakes were taped to frosted
windowpanes. The radiators clanked and steamed.
She went to the cloakroom to hang her hooded coat,
and that's where he was, her red-headed tormentor,
waiting to kick the backs of her knees and call her
stupid. He was an ear wiggler, a knuckle cracker,
a kid who picked his crusty nostrils, one the principal
called a wiseacre. Once when she'd sewn her Girl Scout
housekeeping badge on upside down, he'd said
she was dumb, clumsy, ugly. She suffered that day,
but sat at her desk imagining how she could stab him
with her safety scissors and how he would cry
all through recess with the others standing around.
He would be a mess of snot and tears and after a while
she'd forgive him because, after all, she was a good girl
and wanted peace, a word which she could correctly spell.
But then he would probably spit in her face or crush
a milk carton on her head at lunch and tell everyone
how she was worthless, worthless. She'd pretend
not to care because, big deal, she already knew that.
Let me tell you how she stood in the girls' room stall,
her socks puddled around her ankles, her eyes brimming
with tears, telling herself how different things would be
when she was a grown-up woman, maybe thirty, yes,
how very different she knew everything would be.

Pink

It's the suffering of little girls,
all that fuss of ruffle and frill.
Once we wished to be pink-lipped and lovely,
to be perfectly tipped teacups,
honey-rimmed on the mouths of men.

In our dreams butterflies erupted
from little ovens, their ragged wings
singed with sunlight and ginger.
Clouds were pink skids, eraser rubs
on a blank, blue horizon.

I blush to think that every trifle
is as soft and simple as bubblegum
or pajamas, to think of all the hours spent
propped on elbows, staring out
pastel curtains luffing in the breeze.

Yet there is a power in pink. Outside
the windows of little girls everywhere
there are brash azaleas
and bright zinnias blazing,
dew-drunk and rioting already.

The Thirsting Hours

At night the little ones drown
in their milky sleep. They slip
beneath this life to swim
in salty dreams.
During those thirsting hours
of eyelid flutter and finger twitch,
they drift in the womb of memory.

In the morning they surface again
to the same grubby language,
to the ashes of song crumbling
from their lips. The children's silted
tongues turn the gritty cogs
of story, return them only
to the shores, to the water's edge.

To Spit and Hone

Granddad's whiskers were in the basin,
and I was sad to see them go.
He was out on the stump, keening his knife,
singing a circle on his old whetstone.
It was the August of thrift
and the yard baked to puzzle pieces,
of root-thirst and wheat stripped to pith.
We'd watched the burred sun plod across the sky
and singe the crops all summer.
The wind returned all our prayers.

Her passing was worse than a ten years' drought.
And it was then that I picked my scabs to find my bones,
and then that I wanted to swallow sawdust and soot,
to rinse my body with ashes and shovels of chaff.
I'd wade the switch grass up through the gully,
lie in the dirt and cry.
When I eased into the current of sleep,
my dreams told me that heaven
was a body of water.

Covenant

You draw the bow of barbed wire,
let me pass through to the pasture,
to you and the other side.
It is a good day to walk
the rusty tallgrass sugared
with snow, to measure your stride
through the timber and swale.
Giving me the lee, you track the wind.

Cockleburs catch the laces of our boots;
snow seeps through. And when a honey locust
snags my cap, you laugh, and it makes me think
of those damp Aprils we hunted bushels of mushrooms,
and how winter offers us different things.
But quail, you say, keep deep cover
on afternoons as cold as this.
We step and wait, step again.
So what's left to do
but heave hedge balls into the ditch
and hope for a covey to rise?

At Twelve

after the photographic portraits by Sally Mann

Their ripening is almost impolite.
Splayed under smears of shade,
these girls give back our gaze,
brazen and unashamed. Hips jut,
nipples pout, the body's split chrysalis
is a fluency of nubile limbs, demure
sweats. As cicadas throb damply
in the turgid Virginia heat,
each one owns her moment.
Under clotheslines dragging
with denim and eyelet lace, pollen
settles on their downy arms,
on their swollen and silent lips.

Consider the Thunder

Its low deliberate appeal,
how it speaks of hunger or danger
or deluge. Every weather
shuns its own burden.

And even the heft of sunlight
shrugged from the sky
settles heavy on the shoulders
of cornstalks and children.

Consider the gifts of wind,
all that makeshift music
and the scribbles of twigs
caught in rainspouts and gutters,
debris tangled in a girl's hair.

Even sleet spits its sharp
anointment onto our upturned
faces and delivers
into our hands
a harsh blessing.

T W O

Wherever the Dancing Is Done

I am a fool. Believe it.
I whirl and wheel
in my barefooted way,
drunk and off-kilter,
hair in my face.

For these moments I am fooled
into believing that I am spun
by the moon, that soon
I'll be spirited away.

But I am bound to this place,
wherever the dancing is done,
left with the wish
to be easy in my body
and the clumsy belief
in flung arms and these dirty feet.

Things Familiar

We grieve only for what we know.

—ALDO LEOPOLD

Those were her cornbread and gravy days,
days she swept the kitchen of all but faith
and thrift. She kept the itch of fire
in the matchsafe, humble potatoes in their bin.
Mornings she stirred her first tonic,
honey and vinegar humming in water.
A spoon turned in the glass.
She put bitter hairpins between her teeth,
twining fingers through her hair.
The hours gone from green to ripe to rot,
tomatoes lined up in the sill.
Bolts of cotton folded under needle,
sewn into the garments of years.
And the gallons of ink soaked
into letters and lists, the sting and lilt of words
fastened to fiber, the most familiar of things.

A Prayer for Intercession

There is comfort in a needle
plunged and drawn,
each stitch a whisper and a hush.
I work to the quilt
that will fill a hollow cradle
with splinters and seams
and prayers spurned.
I mend and rip and mend again.

Every aproned lady sweeping in the sun
remembers her dough sleeps in the crock.
They drop their brooms to tuck and pat
four brown bellies in a row.
I watch them carry their warm, heavy loaves
as I stand knee-deep in August and afternoon,
holding buckets of turnips and walnut hulls.

I want a sweet potato baby
with podded pea toes.
I want to hold her
in my crooked, spooned arms,
rock her in my hips,
my empty bowl.

Aurelia Waiting

It was not a bad place, this place, her home.
From a swell above town she watched
brisk bluestem washed in wistful breeze
and Union Pacific shuttle and grind
between county elevators
taking on grain and ambition.
She could have, should have left.

When she was younger, she stretched on her belly
over the riverbank to seine those darting minnows.
Later, she could gut a fish—
just scale and slice and scoop it—
no wonder at all.
She could damn her twisting dirt road
and every place that it led her,
but there was plenty of good to be had.
Her days spun with shade
and waiting for the kettle whistle.
And she waited for fat pods to burst
and send their milkweed message,
for crabapple blossoms and tender rain.

But when the wind would sift the shafts of winter wheat,
she was sure she should have gone.
The stubble fields seemed bitter when she dug
deep in her pocket for the fist of seeds
to fling to the dull birds.
There was always the rusted water pump
and section of rotted fence.
Always and again something
to keep her.

Nemaha County Nocturne

The difficult stars parse the night into silence,
benediction, dream. Between soil and silo thrums
the grammar of grain and all of Kansas rests.

The slender roots of weeds suck at the dirt,
and the listing windmills and ruined barns
lean toward their beginnings. Flowing north,

our river glides through glacial cuts
and those ghosts of primitive sea.
A turtle, overturned dish

of flesh and patience, swims
against history's blur.
Locusts resurrect

the wind and with
reluctant tongues
we name it

holy
holy.

Homestead

He had the wanderfoot,
and that's how we landed
in this harvest of rocks and wind.
We had dirt and water
and some sticks of wood.
We had two earth rooms
and babies in a trundle bed.

At night his hands were shale
resting in the furrow of my back.
And the wind, a plow coming from the west,
turned up the gray clods of our dreams.
Days piled like stones lifted
and placed by the side of the field,
yet whole acres were ahead.
We wondered how west was west,
how we'd come this far.

She wants to be small,
like something left on a bureau:
a fingernail paring, a zinc penny,
a rotted milk tooth, a fleck of dust.

In her room, the walls are porous—
absorbing talcum, sweating lavender.
And as dusk is coaxed into
deeper gray, the shadows stretch,
then disappear,
melding with the dark.

In her kitchen, she feels
like a bowl of wax fruit.
She is a plastic orange,
never peeled.
There is pickling lime
in her pantry, pushed behind
dusty Mason jars that wait
for their scalding.

On her porch, she is a woman
listening to the swing chain creak,
steaming mug of coffee on her knee.
She wishes she could rest
beneath the blistered paint,
burrow into the floorboards.
This is what she wants.

Almanac

There is a physics to burnt toast and tenderness—
a law proven in a kitchen south of a certain town.
Here she scrapes black crumbs in washboard rhythm
for the old man choked with bacon grease
and egg yolk who sits at her table.
Brush of silver whiskers, he leaves,
carrying his body like a sack of feed.
Baked bread and bleach claim this place
where she sits to husk and churn—
each day an adage.

In town, her girdle binds as she markets
for flour and spools of thread.
Weather talks barometric pressure,
rain gauge banter.
Straw purse clasped, she winds home
to the bud and shed, vine and prune.
He is there, driving
the John Deere in wide circles.
And sure as the moon will wax and wane,
the old man pats her bottom,
sits at her table as she ladles stew.

Remedy

She had the remedy for a dead seed,
any sorry thing that could ail a girl.
They knew the way to her sagging porch,
to her window divining light.
Cabbage folds for poultice,
buckthorn to purge,
every pod and petal drawn to soothe.

But her words were like kindling,
snapping and small,
when she wanted her tongue
to run with salve,
to butter their burn
and save them all.

If she could whittle bones from birch
and mold moss for flesh,
she could harvest a woman
from any crooked row.
She would gather baskets of comfrey,
borrow the breeze,
sluice their rot,
make them hers.

Sonnet for Dissonance

The bell's dull clapper stirs each day at noon,
but I want silver lyric, twisted tin,
metal, a jangle of knives and forks in
kitchen sinks, litany of serving spoons.
Ring out chain links and jewelry's jingling tune.
Give me the chime of dimes in slot machines
and the chatter of tacks in hardware bins,
paper clips, and clinking, clanging ruin.

Heaven, I wish you would heap down your scrap,
every cast-off, beat-up, dissonant thing.
I want to hear skeleton keys clatter
and the rain on galvanized washtubs ping.
Let's salvage every melody gone flat.
Let all the graceless and unworthy sing.

Threshing

Under the polished spokes of the sun,
they sickle and sheave their wheat.
He sings her that song
she's been wanting to hear
of riffling water and sweet fall breeze.
But these are her hands calloused with rhythm,
this is her hair full of sweat and chaff.
She braids her body through the rows,
reaping his voice and the autumn seed.

On this day she will leave the field,
leave the husk of her self.
She will rise to praise the harvest moon,
the spirit of soil, wind and rain.
On this night she will lie with her man
and remember the boots under their bed.
They will weave their limbs and twine their dreams
and bless each other with their breath.
In sleep they will grow together,
root, stalk, and grain.

About Rose Ida

Who would give a good god damn
if she walked to town with her two bare feet?
She could comb through her curls
with mulberry-stained fingertips,
and rush into the drugstore,
hike up her skirts and do a jig.
Maybe she would search her nutmeg cupboards
for bones and flasks
and sit, wine-drunk and weepy
on her front steps singing
to her chickens. She might
reach up to the sky as stark
as prairie in winter, call for rain,
rapture.

Supplications to the Blessed Mother

All evening the furnace spun its woolly heat
and the dull pendulum swung.
Sleeping in bloodless sheets, I dreamt
the bedclothes had been stripped and burned,
and I had sewn my own lips together,
stitched my eyelids shut.
It was then that you came to me—
a kind-eyed lady at my window,
a loose grace caught
in the chicken wire of my dreams.

In the kitchen the curtains leak vanilla light
as I lick burnt sugar from each fingertip,
hoping to find them pricked by some dread
spindle, the visitation of night.
What hope is in a rotten apple to be cored
or a rusty pot brought to boil?

Sturdy sunflowers gossip in the ditch,
thrive along the section road,
but my garden is sparse
and the rain will not come.
Holy Mary, in your mercy,
hear and answer me.

Sometimes I sleep in burlap and damp hay
and wake to the rafters of the barn,
to all the pails of cream spilt in the dirt
and the thick milk bottles broken.
I stare up at the swallows skeining our sorrow
and know that what I desire I do not deserve.
But always my prayers get trapped
between these teeth
and this clabbered tongue.

Take away the stone
from my throat and loosen
my knotted breath.
Forgive me for all
I have not done.
I'll shake the cornsilk from my skirts
and go out to meet the day.

I want to push a cart across the countryside,
barefoot and blithe,
peddling shoe polish and shining pots
to farmers and their wives.
I'd call out my love of vegetables,
the virtue of radish and cabbage,
and the beauty of tomatoes tight in their skins.
I want bounty to sprout from the cracks of my palms,
grace to gather in these hands.

I dream split pods lay at my feet
and peas roll off my fingers,
tumble into my lap.
I dream of a table's plenty
and the platter passed steaming, heavy,
heavy hangs over my head.
I dream I feed a baby rhubarb leaves.
This child is me.

Sleep and wake; dream and speak;
seed and rind; pulp and vine.
Give us peace, mother and moon,
mother of us all.

THREE

Backroad

I remember that first whiskey kiss,
desire clambering up the ladder of my ribs.
My hair was wreathed in woodsmoke
and the soft crush of leaves.
I wore his flannel coat every day that winter.

Driving those backroads, I could count
the lazy bales slumped in the snow,
each fencepost strung with barbed wire
till we found our place in the windbreak,
where breath was our own kind of weather.

Across the acres of corn stubble and stars,
our folks slept in the depths of their quilts.
The clocks in our kitchens trembled at the hour,
while we left warmth in the wake of our hands.

Come spring the thaw ran the ruts of the road
and our stand of cottonwoods began to bud.
And on a night riven by lightning,
we gave in to the rhythm of rain.
After, with the truck stuck up to the axle,
he sent me, storm-blind and aching, through the field.
I remember hope, slender as a grass blade,
and guilt, caught like a thorn in my throat.

Commotions of the Flesh

after a line from Epicurus

To live in the world
is to live in the body,
that deepest heap of wants.

To hell with the mind
and its pursuit of its own
proper good. I am concerned here

with the commotions of the flesh.
Living in the fissure between desire
and the having, I have failed,

failed, failed to control myself.
From tooth to tongue, gullet to gut,
I have taken in the religion

of pork chop and gin, tasted
red meat and confection,
nectarine and absinthe.

And I have been pulled along
by the wild vein-song of sex,
the hunger that coils in the blood.

My children sing out to me
from their hammock between my hips;
they coax my fingers to touch.

Forgive me my weaknesses,
for bleeding and sweating and snoring,
for giving in to gravity's tug.

Forgive my shivering, these tears,
this stomach rumble and bone-racket,
this agitation of the willful heart.

Elegy for the Living

There are no words
in the slow language of grief,
only hollow syllables
in this long silence.
We blink and breathe.

We carry around our sadness
like suitcases full of damp clothes.
All the latches have rusted shut.
The hinges ache and creak
with what we do not say.

But what can we say about loss?
Absence has its own life.
We listen when it speaks.

Aubade

Once again we stumble out
of sheet tangle and the dross of dreams.
Daylight comes in little sips
over the lip of the bitter cup.
It is enough to sustain us.
It is enough to know that
we will go out again
with all our failings and loose change,
dazzled and hopeful
in the splendor of the sun.

The Fugitive Eve

In the first moments of knowing,
juice drips down her chin onto
her breasts. Lips and tongue learn
in this oldest, truest way.
The fruit is round and radiant.
The firm weight of it feels
like power. Shreds of flesh catch
in her teeth, and as she eats
she knows it is good.

He needs no serpent to tempt him.
He just wants what she has, just as she wants him
to want what she holds in her hands.
They share it, then toss the core into a bush,
knowing that this is the beginning of death,
the first and best blessing.

And with the original chill of delight
and shame, she is on the lam,
running through brambles, plum boughs
and luminous webs, past low-slung branches,
past the birds of the air and beasts of the field,
over the rocky soil, stumbling out
of the garden, out of the numb perfection
of before into the brilliant and difficult ever-after.
She is running and running, she feels
the warm rub of her blood-slicked thighs
and a thudding, which is her heart. He is close
behind her, clutching the pain in his side.
They take hold of one another
in their wonder and woe,
and we call out to them
from our place in the future,

this moment, now. We beg them
with our fragile voices,
Mother, Father, bear us
into the beautiful trouble
of this world.

Rhythm

I trust the heart,
   little tinder box in my chest,
   the steady burn at neck and wrist,
but what about breath,
   those feeble bellows I pump
   again, again?
In sleep, what if I forget?

At Cather's Grave

Veiled in deep New Hampshire pine,
you rest in a bed of mast and loam.
A pilgrim from the plains, I've come in homage
to your open-skied and earth-turned words.
Monadnock will not shadow you.

We both know that the prairie
is like a page, our living and dying
written in every tuck and swell.
I wish we could walk out together,
arms linked, toward the sun-doused sedge.

But everywhere, whether here
or there, the wind stories us
and the land will take us in.
We are all happy to be dissolved
into something so complete and great.

Burning Back

Once I was a girl with a truck
and a tackle box full of jigs and treble hooks.
We sat on my tailgate to watch pasture scorch,
and he traced my bones—hip, thigh, shin.

I cross the county line at dusk,
drive west past silos
toward that thick rope of smoke.
It is spring and time for prairie to burn.
So I pull off, get out to breathe in April
and to watch tallgrass swept to char.
Each blade the fire takes
will return richer still.

I stand at this edge of fallow field,
and the swells blaze yellow, then red.
Like a brittle weed I want to know again
the prairie's need to burn and burn.

At Twenty-Eight

It seems I get by on more luck than sense,
not the kind brought on by knuckle to wood,
breath on dice, or pennies found in the mud.
I shimmy and slip by on pure fool chance.
At turns charmed and cursed, a girl knows romance
as coffee, red wine, and books; solitude
she counts as daylight virtue and muted
evenings, the inventory of absence.
But this is no sorry spinster story,
just the way days string together a life.
Sometimes I eat soup right out of the pan.
Sometimes I don't care if I will marry.
I dance in my kitchen on Friday nights,
singing like only a lucky girl can.

Epithalamion for a Maiden Aunt

Enjoy life with one you love for all the fleeting days
that are granted you under the sun,
all your fleeting days.

—ECCLESIASTES 9:7–9

After the long, Lenten penance of winter,
your forty-three-year fast is broken.
The churchyard offers a fragrance
that is like ripe fruit or our want of it—
baskets of apples, soft pears, the sweet
contradiction of apricot flesh, plush skin,
tart pit. The spirea blossoms are frothing,
bridal white, and from the steeple a call
bells out across the pasture where cattle
chew the tender grasses with vigor.
Love is a revenant come round at last.
Take the hand of your loved one, this day,
your husband, and find comfort there.
Find whatever is eternal, vernal, joyful
and wed it. Tithe yourselves ten times
to the other's care. And when you take
your turn in the muslin-rustling waltz,
encircled and humming in this vocation,
remember the music that led you here.

Jazz Rhapsody

for Michael Jefry Stevens

Wrap round that bracelet of song,
each note a liquid jewel
that lingers at the turn of a wrist—
amber tone, jasper rest,
ivory trill. Such bright music
adorns our pulse points
as your piano sends its garnet
secrets to nest in our ears.
And always with a sage's grace,
you spin out this finest, silver tune.

The Wound You Need

Piss drunk outside Port Arthur we pitched rocks
into the bayou, wrecked its green stillness
with every hurl. From the truck dash Janis,
her voice full of tatters and ash, told us
what we already believed we understood,
that sometimes it's the wound you need
to heal yourself. And on the raggedy
crust edge of Texas, we compared scars.

Sometimes it was all we could do to haul
our bones to the state line, to the sweet safety
of sun-up and runny eggs for breakfast.
We mopped our plates with store-bought bread
and fell into bed at noon. When we woke
we were jagged for it, the hiss of gin over ice,
another tired night of big talk and bar fights.
Tell me, how many times did we promise

to mend our ways? At least a thousand times
a thousand, and I'm not even sorry
anymore. Every mess I've made is mine.
Rummaging around the glove box, I found
that old map, soft from fumbling and folding,
with a crease right down through the town
where we lived. That was long ago, my friend,
but you can still get there from here.

What Endures

Over the seventh hill of Prague the sun
tamps out and twilight's net is tossed down.
I hear the trees mutter their sparrow vespers
as a sooty nimbus settles above the city's statues.
Cherubs garland cornice and frieze;
they wait: golem, griffin, and dour saint.
Even the Infant Child extends his tiny hands
in the dimming church of Our Lady Victorious.

Back home pinched stars shatter then weep
over the pastures and backyards of Kansas.
In lawn chairs the folks murmur and sigh
while children gesture and prance, signing their names
against the night in wild sparkling arcs.
For a moment their images ghost the air.
Even now they wonder what endures,
lighting another little torch in the dark.

The Progress of Night

In the late elegiac light, insects
    chide the frail contraption of the sky,
        its faulty system of pulleys and wires.

Piteous stars circuit the stripped gears
    of galaxy as crickets keep grinding
        out twilight's tinny, dwindling music.

Again that pale immigrant blunders in
    to watch over the progress of night,
        to observe the grim magics we practice,

all the oaths we take and make and utter.
    What comfort can we offer another
        traveler under this same unsteady scaffold?

We'll find no charm against calamity.
    Though the dark architecture of the heart
        is buttressed by sternum, girded by ribs,

we build our lives from its very trembling.